BARK

BY
STEPHANIE DICKSON

Published by Playdead Press 2021

© Stephanie Dickson 2021

Stephanie Dickson has asserted her rights under the Copyright, Design and Patents Act, 1988, to be identified as the author of this work.

A CIP catalogue record for this book is available from the British Library.

ISBN 978-1-910067-92-5

Caution

All rights whatsoever in this play are strictly reserved and application for performance should be sought through the author before rehearsals begin. No performance may be given unless a license has been obtained.

This book is sold subject to the condition that it shall not by way of trade or otherwise, be lent, resold, hired out, or otherwise circulated without the publisher's prior consent in any form of binding or cover other than that in which it is published and without a similar condition including this condition being imposed on the subsequent purchaser.

Playdead Press
www.playdeadpress.com

The first performance of **BARK** was at the Old Red Lion Theatre on Tuesday 3rd August 2021 with the following cast:

GRACE	**Stephanie Dickson**
HELEN	**Sarah Somerville**

CREATIVES:

Director	**Joseph Blake**
Writer	**Stephanie Dickson**
Choreographers	**Jordan Mills & Bobbie Cadden**
Graphic Designer	**Ben Westcott**
Sound & Lighting	**Daniel Peart & Gabriella Coomber**
Photographer	**Victoria Dickson**
Consultant	**Dr Richard Phillips, MB BChir**

To my parents, Elizabeth & David, without whom nothing I do would be possible.

With special thanks to Dr Richard Phillips, MB BChir and The Old Red Lion Theatre.

CHARACTERS:

GRACE: 18 from South London. Grace has Stage III Acute Lymphoblastic Leukaemia (ALL). She is positive, upbeat and outgoing. She was first diagnosed at the age of 5 and the leukaemia was treated, only for it to return now which is why she is in the private hospital. Her main goals in life are to enjoy herself and live life to the full.

HELEN: 65, from Oxford originally but moved to South East London following her divorce. She has a son, Brett who is 33. She has Lung Cancer and has been in the private hospital receiving radiotherapy and some chemotherapy for 5-6 months. She is normally quite reserved, well-mannered and keeps herself to herself.

SCENE 1

We are in the TV room of a hospital. It has been decorated for Christmas. There are two seats side-by-side next to a coffee table. At the back of the stage, there is a counter with an assortment of kitchen items, including a kettle, tea, coffee, biscuits and plates. These are all real, for the actors to utilise as they wish.

GRACE (18) sits in one of the chairs facing the TV.

After a while, HELEN (65) enters. They have never met before. There is an awkwardness and hesitancy between them.

HELEN busies herself in the kitchen area. The pair do not speak.

The sounds of a NATURE DOCUMENTARY begin to play on the TV. HELEN decides to sit down to watch it. She sits in the chair next to GRACE.

NATURE DOCUMENTARY CONTINUES TO PLAY

GRACE: Do dogs think in barks?

HELEN: ...Sorry?

GRACE: Do you reckon that dogs think in barks?

HELEN: What?

GRACE: Well when I think it's in English. Dogs don't speak English, obviously, but they have thoughts, don't they? So... do they think in barks?

HELEN: I can't... I mean...

GRACE: Yeah?

HELEN: I have no idea.

GRACE: Yeah, neither do I.

They fall back into silence.

HELEN: So what about cats?

GRACE: Well exactly. And penguins?!

HELEN: I wish I knew.

GRACE: So do I.

PAUSE

What noise do penguins make?

HELEN: I was just wondering that!

GRACE: I feel like I've heard it but I just can't hear it in my head right now.

HELEN: I think it's like (*makes a strange 'penguin' noise*)

GRACE: (*LAUGHING*) No, it's more like (*makes her own strange noise*)

They laugh.

HELEN: What time is it?

GRACE: 3:30.

HELEN: I should probably get going soon.

GRACE: Oh, yeah.

HELEN gets up and tidies away everything she has been using.

HELEN: See you, then.

GRACE: What? Oh yeah, see you.

HELEN: It was lovely to meet you.

GRACE: You too... er, sorry, what's your name?

HELEN: Oh, it's Helen. Yours?

GRACE: Grace. I've not seen you in here before. How long have you been here?

HELEN: Oh, well, with the rests, around about 5 or 6 months. You?

GRACE: In and out since I was 5.

HELEN: Bloody hell.

GRACE: Tell me about it.

HELEN is torn between her need to leave and wanting to speak to GRACE.

HELEN: So, do you see many people?

GRACE: Yeah, I see mum and dad all the time, and I've got a ton of aunties and cousins that come and visit. My mates, they come over a lot too. My best mate, Jess, she's here all the time, she's great. What about you?

HELEN: Oh, just my son, really.

GRACE: Ah, what's his name?

HELEN: Brett.

GRACE: Brett. That's a cool name. How old is he?

HELEN: Oh, he's not that much older than you I'd say, he's 33.

GRACE: What?! I'm only 18!

HELEN: Seriously? Wow, I thought you were older!

They fall back into an awkward silence. HELEN needs to leave.

GRACE: I'm actually nearly 19 though. I turn 19 in January, so not long now! I'll be out of here by then.

HELEN: Will you?

GRACE: Yeah, I'm gonna be out for Christmas.

HELEN: Good for you.

PAUSE.

GRACE: Don't you need to go?

HELEN: Well, yes I… actually no. No. I could probably stay a bit longer.

GRACE: Cool. You gonna come and sit back down?

HELEN: Yes, why not?

HELEN sits back down. The pair resume watching TV.

GRACE: I think I'd be good at that.

HELEN: What's that now?

GRACE: Presenting. I'd love to be famous. I think I'm bubbly enough without being really annoying, you know? I reckon I'd be like Holly Willoughby and Phillip Schofield. They're like your mates that you'd go down the pub with, aren't they? Everyone likes them.

HELEN: Oh yes, I love them. Especially that Philip. So, what would you present?

GRACE: That's the thing really, all the good stuff is already taken by either Holly and Pip or Ant and Dec. I'm not sure I'd get a look in.

HELEN: Tricky.

GRACE: I think I'd need another person, really. It seems to work so well for those lot because they bounce off each other, you know? They're, like, a double act.

HELEN: It worked for French and Saunders.

GRACE: Who?

HELEN: Oh, never mind.

GRACE: Maybe you could be my presenting partner?

HELEN: Me! God. Well now, there's a thought.

GRACE: What do you do?

HELEN: I work in a bank.

GRACE: Oh really? Which one?

HELEN:	Lloyds.
GRACE:	Ah, shame, I'm with Santander.
HELEN:	Oh.

ANOTHER PAUSE.

They continue to watch TV, eating their biscuits and drinking their tea.

GRACE:	Did you always want to work in a bank?
HELEN:	Um, no, actually. I used to want to be a policewoman.
GRACE:	Really? Wow! That's so cool! What made you change your mind?
HELEN:	Well, um. Nothing, really. I just didn't.
GRACE:	Oh. Well you still could.
HELEN:	I think it's a bit late for that, love.
GRACE:	Of course it's not! Actually, I have a theory about this.
HELEN:	Go on.
GRACE:	Okay, so I've always said that when people get really old, like 40, they get all boring and stop caring about having fun and what they look like and stuff like that.

SHE PAUSES, taking in HELEN'S expression.

        Sorry, no offence.

HELEN: None taken, I guess. Anyway, your theory?

GRACE: Yeah, so I was thinking that we should all have to stick to what we wanted to be when we were little and try and make it work somehow. So whatever we said we wanted to be when we were, like, 8 or something. Like when I was in school, I used to want to be Hermione Granger when I grew up... oh sorry, do you know who that is?

HELEN: ...Yes, love.

GRACE: Right, yeah, well I wanted to be her, so I would have to make that work somehow. Which is kind of hard, because I'm not really clever. Or magic. Or Emma Watson.

HELEN: I think there might be a flaw in that theory of yours.

GRACE: Well it might work for other people. Like what did you want to be, before the policewoman?

HELEN: What do you mean?

GRACE: Like, when you were really young, like... primary school.

HELEN: Wow, what I wanted to be in primary school?

GRACE: Yeah, like that's if you can even remember, I know it was a long time ago.

HELEN gives her a stern look.

GRACE: What? Oh, sorry.

HELEN: I can actually remember what I wanted to be when I was about 5 or 6, thank you very much.

GRACE: Go on.

HELEN: Well... if I'm *completely* honest...

GRACE: Yeah?

HELEN: I wanted to be a… a frog.

GRACE: A frog?! What?! Why?!

THEY LAUGH.

HELEN: I don't know! They just seemed so happy and free. Jumping around all the time. I went out to this pond with my Dad a lot and I remember thinking that it looked like a really good life, bouncing around.

GRACE: Well, Helen, if you want to be a frog, you be a frog.

HELEN: Do you know what, Grace? I might just do that.

GRACE: And then you can tell me if you think in ribbits and we'll finally know the answer!

HELEN: *(LAUGHING)* I promise. I really should go now. Will you be in here tomorrow?

GRACE: I'm not sure.

HELEN: Oh. Well, I can come and find you, if you like.

GRACE: That would be great! I'm Leukaemia. You?

HELEN: Lung cancer. It was lovely to meet you, Grace.

GRACE: Bark Bark Bark!

The lights fade out.

FIVE YEARS TIME BY NOAH AND THE WHALE PLAYS.

SCENE 2

A movement sequence begins in which we see HELEN and GRACE going about their day-to-day lives in the hospital in different segments. Each segment is bookended with the music and lighting to show that time is passing inside the hospital. Each one shows a different aspect of their friendship and lives.

FIVE YEARS TIME BY NOAH AND THE WHALE CONTINUES TO PLAY.

<u>SEGMENT ONE:</u>

LIGHTS UP.

HELEN sits in the TV room, a crossword puzzle on her lap. She is half doing it and half watching the TV.

GRACE enters.

HELEN: Oh. Hello again. Grace, was it?

GRACE: Yeah, that's right. What was your name again?

HELEN: Helen.

GRACE: Oh yeah, that was it. My friend had a cat that was called Helen.

HELEN: Oh?

GRACE: Yeah, the cat's dead now.

HELEN: Oh.

HELEN nods awkwardly.

GRACE: What are you watching?

HELEN: Well, I'm not entirely sure, I'm not really watching it. It's some sort of gameshow I think. Lots of attractive young couples in swimwear getting up to all sorts.

GRACE: Oh yeah, I've seen that before! It's awful, isn't it?

HELEN: Oh it is. Awful.

They both look at each other. GRACE glances around the room to check that they're alone.

GRACE: Wanna watch some more?

HELEN: Definitely!

Giggling, GRACE comes and sits next to HELEN, in the same chair that she was sitting in yesterday. They both begin to watch the show, grinning at each other.

GRACE: Would you ever go on a show like that?

HELEN: Me? With all of my wobbly bits? Chance would be a fine thing!

GRACE: Well I would.

HELEN: Yeah?

GRACE: Yeah. I'd love to be famous.

HELEN: Oh yes, you did say.

GRACE: Where were you the other day?

HELEN: Hmm?

GRACE: I thought you were going to come over and visit.

HELEN: Oh yes, I did think about it, but…

GRACE: What?

HELEN: Oh I don't know. We'd only just met and…

GRACE: And?

HELEN: Well. I guess I just didn't want to be a nuisance. That's all.

GRACE: Nah, you wouldn't have been. You would have been a life-saver.

HELEN: Oh really?

GRACE: Yeah. They took a bunch of tests.

HELEN: Oh, I hate that.

GRACE: Oh don't even, I feel like a bloody pin cushion, the amount of needles they keep sticking in me. I'm bruising loads as well, 'cos they can never find a vein. I feel like suing.

HELEN: Sorry, love. I'll definitely come by another time.

GRACE: Promise?

HELEN: Promise.

GRACE: So. Shitty reality TV shows and animal documentaries. That's what you like to watch?

HELEN: So it would seem.

GRACE: Oh, I like all the whodunnit stuff, and the detective shows. I really like that Luther, have you ever seen that?

HELEN: Oh, I'm not sure, what one's that?

GRACE: It's proper scary, it's the one with that well fit guy, he's a detective, can't remember the character's name, but he's got that proper manly voice and he's all rough, and he's all like 'Alice, Alice' and I'm just like, hell yeah, I'll be your Alice. And it's got that girl in it, you know the one, with the eyebrows?

HELEN: Sorry, I'm not sure.

GRACE: I'll show you sometime. I'm sure it's on Netflix.

HELEN: That's sweet. Thank you, love. Something else to add to the list!

GRACE: Do you watch TV so much because you're stuck in here with nothing else to do?

HELEN looks very taken aback.

GRACE: What?

HELEN: Nothing... nothing, that was just very... well, people don't normally talk about it.

GRACE: I know, I don't get it. Like yeah, we're in here for a reason, why is everyone avoiding it?

HELEN: I suppose you're right.

GRACE: I know.

GRACE grins at HELEN. They go back to watching TV.

LIGHTS FADE OUT.

SEGMENT TWO:

LIGHTS UP.

GRACE lies in the chair in the TV room, asleep, holding her phone as though she was waiting for a call when she fell asleep.

HELEN enters. She spots GRACE and stops. She takes off her shawl and puts it over GRACE like a blanket. She leaves.

LIGHTS FADE OUT.

SEGMENT THREE:

LIGHTS UP.

HELEN stands in the middle of the stage, holding GRACE'S phone. They are bickering playfully, trying to FaceTime BRETT.

HELEN: I pressed it! Brett? Can you see me?

GRACE: You need to flip it!

HELEN: I did! Look, press!

GRACE: Flip it! Press there, not there, look, now you've exited it! He can't see you!

HELEN: I can't hear him.

HELEN holds the phone to her ear.

Brett?

GRACE: You don't put it to your ear! Now he can only see inside your ear!

HELEN: Stop shouting!

GRACE: Give it here!

HELEN: I'll just call him. Brett? I'll call you!

GRACE: Just give it!

LIGHTS FADE OUT.

SEGMENT FOUR

LIGHTS UP.

HELEN sits in her chair, reading a book. The TV is off. GRACE enters.

GRACE: Alright, Hel, how's it going?

HELEN: Good.

GRACE: Yeah? You sure?

HELEN: Uh-huh.

GRACE: Right. Okay...

GRACE goes to sit down next to her, unnerved by HELEN'S quietness.

GRACE: So, what have you been doing?

HELEN: Nothing.

GRACE: Fair enough.

GRACE plays with her phone for a bit, but she is obviously concerned and uncomfortable with HELEN'S silence.

GRACE: What are you reading?

HELEN sighs and shows her the title of the book. It is a book about self-help. GRACE shrugs.

GRACE: Bad day then?

HELEN: Bad day.

GRACE nods. She begins to watch videos on her phone. One of them is of a TV show that is very loud and vulgar. GRACE is giggling at it.

HELEN: Grace.

GRACE: What?

HELEN: Could you keep it down? I've just started a new cycle of treatment and my brain feels like it's going to burst.

GRACE looks taken aback and is offended.

GRACE: Fine then. If that's the way you want to be.

GRACE puts the phone down, sulking.

So what other side effects do you have?

HELEN: Oh for God's sake, feeling sick, headache, tired, muscle pain, not wanting to talk, just wanting to sleep.

GRACE: Is one of the side effects that you become a total bitch?

HELEN and GRACE glare at each other. Then HELEN smiles weakly.

HELEN: Yes, I think so.

GRACE smiles at HELEN.

GRACE: I'm sorry. I know its shit.

HELEN smiles at her meekly and then returns to her book. The pair sit in a comfortable silence for a bit. GRACE eventually stands.

> Well, I think I might go for a nap. I think you need one as well to be honest.

HELEN: Cheeky sod.

GRACE: Always. Right, see you later.

HELEN: Uh-huh.

GRACE leaves the room, leaving HELEN fighting not to fall asleep in the chair. She struggles to move, her whole body in pain.

HELEN: *(TO HERSELF)* I can't deal with this.

LIGHTS FADE OUT.

SEGMENT FIVE

LIGHTS UP

GRACE and HELEN sit in their chairs, but they have moved them to face one other. HELEN looks visibly better than she did in the previous scene.

There is a Chess board in-between them. HELEN is teaching GRACE how to play.

GRACE: So, do you live near here?

HELEN: Near the hospital?

GRACE: Yeah.

HELEN: Fairly near, yes. I'm in South East. You can't do that.

GRACE: Why not?

HELEN: You can only move it twice the first time.

GRACE: That makes no sense. Hold up, did you say South East?

HELEN: Yes. I've just taken your rook now, do you see? You should have put that there.

GRACE: You can't be South East.

HELEN: Yes, I am.

GRACE: You're deffo too posh to be South East.

HELEN: Posh?!

GRACE: *(COPYING HELEN'S ACCENT)* 'Posh!'

HELEN: I'll take that as a compliment. But I'm by no means posh.

GRACE: Did you live somewhere else before? Can I do a big L with this?

HELEN: Show me?

GRACE shows her, moving her knight.

HELEN: Yes you can. And yes I did, I used to live in Oxford.

GRACE: Oxford! I knew it! That's like the poshest place in the world!

HELEN: Check.

GRACE: Shit! How did you do that?

HELEN: Well, you moved your knight there, and here's my bishop, you see?

GRACE: Ugh. You need twenty eyes to do this.

HELEN: You'll get it.

GRACE: Doubt it. I don't understand why the whole thing is centered around the King anyway, he's bloody useless.

HELEN: That's just the way it is, I'm afraid.

GRACE: Not if I have anything to do with it.

HELEN: Do you know, I think you could change the world, Grace.

GRACE: Oh, definitely. If I ever get out of here.

HELEN: You will. You're going to be out for Christmas remember? That's what you told me.

GRACE: Yeah, I did say that, didn't I? It's my favourite time of year. It'd be cool to be out of here before then, though. I'm missing so much shit.

HELEN: Like what?

GRACE: Like parties. Days out. Bottomless brunches. Getting Married. Having kids.

HELEN: Married and kids at your age?

GRACE: Yeah, loads of people I went to school with are. You just scroll through Facebook or Insta and you can see all of their pictures. Fiona in the year above has already had four! She just had another baby with her new guy, Jay. She met him at college. The baby is well ugly.

HELEN: Grace!

GRACE: What? It's true.

HELEN: Even so. Still, you don't need to worry about all of that right now. You'll get your chance.

GRACE: Yeah. Thing is, with everything, I haven't done much since school really.

HELEN: Well a lot of people say that school days are the best of your life.

GRACE: Really?

HELEN: Yup.

GRACE: That's well sad.

HELEN: They were the best days of my life.

GRACE: Seriously? But what about all the stuff that comes after? Living with your mates, or getting your own place. What about getting a cool job, dating, all that sort of thing?

HELEN: It's not quite that glamorous I'm afraid. Or at least, it wasn't for me.

GRACE: But why not?

HELEN: Well, I wasn't too sure what I wanted to do. I'd grown out of wanting to be a frog then, that's for sure. I got a waitressing job, you know, to tide me over. That's when I met Rick.

GRACE: Rick? Is that your husband?

HELEN: Was.

GRACE: Oh shit, sorry Hel! Did he die?

HELEN: Die? Heavens, no. We got divorced, love.

GRACE: Oh. My friend Amy's parents got divorced when we was in year eight.

HELEN: Yes, Brett was much older than that, fortunately.

GRACE: Is that why you moved to London?

HELEN: Yes, exactly. At first it was me and Brett, but I've been on my own for a while now. I was thinking about moving closer to him, spend more time together, you know, but then...

GRACE: But then you got ill.

HELEN: But then I got ill. Lung cancer. And I've not smoked a day in my life! How's that for luck? But still, I can't complain really. Brett paid for me to go private, you know, come here.

GRACE: But can't you just get surgery or something? Pop it out, like that scene from that film, Alien! You know the one, where he's lying like that and the thing bursts out of his chest like...

GRACE begins demonstrating the scene, being extremely loud and graphic.

HELEN: *(looking VERY SICK)* Grace. Please.

GRACE: Sorry.

HELEN: But no, unfortunately not. Previous health issues. So, radio it is.

GRACE: Tell me about it. It's pretty shit.

HELEN: Yes, indeed. Check mate.

GRACE: Can we play something else now?

HELEN: Like what?

GRACE: I was thinking poker.

HELEN: Do you know how to play?

GRACE: Yup. Jess got me a set. She went to this really cool pub tournament and so she got me it to practice, so that when I get out, we can go to one together.

HELEN: How exciting. Will I get to meet her soon?

GRACE: Well, you know how it is. She's really busy. But I'm sure she'll visit soon. She was meant to be coming by next week, actually. There's this big Christmas party coming up with literally everyone I know, and I'm hoping my doctor will let me go. It's just for the night, but I've been looking forward to it for ages.

HELEN: Ah well, I hope you get to go.

GRACE: I'll tell you all about it, don't worry. I'll go and get the poker, yeah?

HELEN: Alright, love.

GRACE exits. HELEN watches after her, worried.

HELEN: Eighteen. And she's worried that she's missing out. Bless her. So young. So, so young. Still, she doesn't act it. Sometimes it's hard to remember that she's been in and out of here for so long. I guess that's being ill. It ages you.

I wish I'd been more like Grace when I was younger. Unapologetic, feisty, strong. She truly believes she can take on the world and win. I think she probably could.

I was never like that. I was too scared of what people would say, what people would think. Always so worried about doing the right thing. That's why I waited so long to marry Rick. We wanted to make sure we had enough money, that we did it all properly, invited everybody and had the perfect, beautiful ceremony. And it was. It was perfect. The perfect day. The perfect life.

And then we got divorced anyway.

Still, I can't complain really. Because if it wasn't for Rick, I wouldn't have had my Brett.

I still remember when I was pregnant with him, as clearly as if it were yesterday. I was scared. So, so scared. I mean, I was 32 at the time, positively ancient to be pregnant back then! A geriatric mother. And having a baby, an unpredictable, messy, dependent thing. How was that going to fit into the life I had? But I needn't have worried. He was, and still is, perfect. I know every mother says that, but he really is. Beautiful, inside and out. And a successful lawyer too! Just what every mother wants. I wouldn't change him for the world.

He can't visit that often, but he does his best. I'm so proud of him.

Grace is trying to pack so much in, so many events and memories and life experiences in such a short time frame. Trying to work down her entire list, one after the other. But then again, why not? Waiting for tomorrow, being careful, planning everything - it didn't work for me. I got cancer anyway. The big C. You always worry that you might hear those words and... well. There we go. And I still haven't got round to half of the list. So maybe I should think about doing things Grace's way. Maybe.

LIGHTS FADE OUT.

SCENE 3

DAVID BOWIE – LIFE IS A CIRCUS PLAYS

LIGHTS FADE UP.

GRACE, who is looking more unwell than we have seen her thus far, walks into the TV room, agitated, upset and angry. She has a piece of paper in her hand that she reads over and over again. Eventually, she balls it up and throws it away. She gets out her phone and sends a message, before sitting back on the chair.

HELEN enters the TV room. She looks excited when she sees GRACE.

HELEN: Hello you! Now listen, I know you didn't quite get the hang of chess, but I was thinking we can give it another go?

GRACE: *(DEJECTEDLY)* No thanks.

HELEN: Oh, okay. Well maybe something else? Or we could watch a film?

GRACE: I'm alright.

HELEN: Has something happened?

GRACE: Yeah.

HELEN: Are you okay?

GRACE: Not really.

HELEN: Do you want to talk about it?

GRACE: It's a long story.

HELEN: I've got time.

HELEN sits down next to GRACE. Eventually, GRACE sighs and begins to share.

GRACE: Well, you know that I mentioned that there was a Christmas party that I wanted to go to? That my friend Jess was going to take me to?

HELEN: I do.

GRACE: And do you remember that I said I was hoping my Doctor would let me go?

HELEN: Oh. I see.

GRACE: She's such a bitch.

HELEN: Who?

GRACE: Doctor Cook, obviously. She's hated me from the moment she met me, I swear.

HELEN: I seriously doubt that, Grace.

GRACE: No, she has, trust me.

HELEN: Which one is she? I might have seen her around.

GRACE: Blonde, tall, walks around like she's got a stick shoved up her arse?

HELEN: *(LAUGHING)* Ah yes, I think I might know.

GRACE: Yeah, her. I told her weeks ago about this party, weeks and weeks ago, like back in October. She knew how much it meant to me, and she made me think I might be able to go. I hate her.

HELEN: I'm sorry, love. Did she say why you can't go?

GRACE: They did a bunch of tests and she was all 'it looks hopeful, all the signs are that it's going in the right direction' and all of this, so I'm, like, planning what I'm going to wear to this party, and *then* she calls me in and says that the treatment wasn't working as well as she'd hoped and so she's 'really sorry', but I really need to stay in the hospital right now. It's SO unfair.

HELEN: Ah. That's a shame, love. Still, I'm sure it's for the best.

GRACE: Pfft, yeah, the best for *her*. I bet she didn't have any intention of letting me go. I bet she just wanted to get my hopes up. It's probs because nobody has ever given her a snog under the mistletoe. I bet she spends Christmas alone with her cats and she's jealous so she's taking it out on me.

HELEN: Oh Grace, I'm sorry. But I don't think she'd make you stay in if it wasn't a concern.

GRACE: I'm just so pissed off.

HELEN: I know, love. Was it a really important party?

GRACE: Yes! Well. No. Not really *important* I guess. It was just this girl from school, Luce, she was hosting it 'cos her dad's away. I didn't even really like her to be honest. She's well full of herself. She's one of those girls that has 'works at Hollister model' on her Facebook and gets her boyfriend to take photos of her posing in her underwear to rack up the likes on insta and pretend she's a model, when really she's just an anorexic with an attitude.

HELEN is visibly shocked at this comment. There is a slight silence.

HELEN: ...Right. Good.

GRACE: Sorry. I didn't mean that. I'm just in a shit mood.

HELEN: Don't worry, love. But if you feel like that then why do you want to go to the party at all?

GRACE: Well, there's a few reasons really. But honestly, Hel? It's because Josh Green is going to be there.

HELEN: Oh? And who is this Josh Green then?

GRACE: He's this totally gorgeous lad who was in the year above me at school. I used to have a thing for him but I haven't seen him since my GCSE's.

HELEN: Ah, I'm sorry, love. Do you really like him?

GRACE: Nah, not really. I've just heard he's a great shag.

HELEN: *(SPLUTTERING)* Sorry?!

GRACE: What? I've been in and out of this shit-hole, haven't I, it's not like I've had the chance to have a proper relationship, is it? Tonight was gonna be the night, Hel. I was gonna go to a party with my mates, and wear a sparkly Christmas outfit and some pathetic antlers that Jess got in Claire's. I was gonna drink that God awful cheap vodka that smells like nail polish, you know the one, and

	get with a fit lad and just have some *fun*. I feel like I'm missing out on everything in here - there's always something happening. The nights out, the festivals, the memories, everything. Like, don't get me wrong, I love my mates and they all come to see me and that, but they get to like, live, you know? Like I'm just a part of their schedule and then they get to go out there and have fun and I just have to sit here. Waiting to get better.
HELEN:	I know.
GRACE:	I had it all figured out you know, Hel.
HELEN:	Yeah?
GRACE:	Yeah. I was going to get really good grades in my GCSE's and then I was going to go to prom with all of mates and my boyfriend at the time, Tom. I haven't told you about Tom yet. We were going out from when I was like, 13 up until just before I came in here. I was gonna lose my virginity to him on prom night too,'cos his parents were away. I wanted to wait until I was 16 and left school, I thought that was the right thing to do. If I'd have known that *this* was gonna happen, I would have just bloody done it. He dumped me when I told him the leukaemia had come back, said he wasn't ready for something so serious. Like HE was the one who had to deal with the life-changing illness. Prick.

HELEN: It's a scary thing, love. And I think you did the right thing. It sounds like he wasn't worth it.

GRACE: Yeah, maybe. But anyway, after that I was gonna go to college and do my A-Levels. Then I was gonna take a year out and spend it working full-time doing, like, receptionist work or something like that, just earn a ton of money, and then I was going to go travelling with Jess. I want to go to Norway and she wants to go to New Zealand so we were just going to do a whole year of travelling the world. Then after that it would be come back, go uni, meet someone, probs get married, the whole shebang.

HELEN: Sounds like you've got it all mapped out.

GRACE: Yeah, well, I did, until my fucking body decided to stop working properly.

HELEN: Well, hopefully you'll still be able to do all of those things.

GRACE: Oh, don't worry, I deffo will. I'm just so bored of waiting to get started! You're so lucky, Hel.

HELEN: Me?!

GRACE: Yeah, how old are you?

HELEN: Well, if you must know, I'm 65.

GRACE: 65? Fuck me, you're, like, an actual pensioner.

HELEN: Excuse me, that's...

GRACE: *(INTERRUPTING)* You've had a whole life already, before this. I'm so jealous, you've already had all the fun.

HELEN: Hmm.

GRACE: What?

HELEN: It's just… thinking about it… I don't think I've had any real fun in a long time.

GRACE: Really? Why?

HELEN: Oh. I don't know, really. I guess that, sometimes, when you get married, you can get all bogged down with daily life, you know?

GRACE: But didn't you and your husband have fun?

HELEN: Oh yes. We used to, years ago.

GRACE: Did you really love him?

HELEN: Yes. I really did, back then.

GRACE: So what about now?

HELEN: Now?

GRACE: Yeah. Is there anyone else?

HELEN: Oh, I don't think so, love.

GRACE: But why not?

HELEN: I think I'm a bit past it now.

GRACE: That's just ridiculous, of course you aren't!

HELEN: That's really kind, Grace, but life doesn't work that way, unfortunately. I had my chance and it didn't work out.

GRACE: But don't you wish you could just try again? Start over?

HELEN: No. I have Brett. That's all that matters.

GRACE: But there are so many options now, Hel. Dating sites, apps. I'll get you on Tinder!

HELEN: Bless you, love, but what would anyone want with me? I'm 65, divorced and not exactly model material.

GRACE: Stop that! You're brilliant and clever and kind and super attractive in that MILF kind of way.

HELEN: I don't even want to know what that means. Thank you, I guess. But even if all that were true and someone could maybe get on board with all of that, there's still the cancer.

THERE'S A SILENCE.

GRACE: Do you think that there's still a chance for us both?

HELEN: I hope so.

GRACE: Tell you what, we'll go away somewhere.

HELEN: What?

GRACE: When we're out of here. You and me. We'll go somewhere hot and sunny and gorgeous – Greece or somewhere. Cheap and cheerful. We can sit by the pool all day and get a nice tan – but we'll have to make sure that we wear suncream, because knowing my luck, I'll get skin cancer and I'll end up back in this dump.

HELEN: *(Laughing, shocked)* Grace! You can't joke about that!

GRACE: Course you can! I'm serious though. We'll spend all day drinking cocktails by the pool or on the beach and then at night we'll go out and get a local bloke called Dennis to do body shots off us.

HELEN: Goodness!

GRACE: Promise we'll do it?

HELEN: Oh I don't think so, love.

GRACE: Come on, Hel, you need to live a bit. Have some fun once in a while, you deserve it.

HELEN: Hmm.

HELEN falls into a thoughtful silence.

GRACE: Anyway, I'm gonna go and get ready for bed. You think about that holiday, yeah?

HELEN: What? Oh. Yeah.

GRACE: Good. Night, Hel.

HELEN: Goodnight, Grace.

GRACE EXITS, leaving HELEN on stage, deep in thought. She looks around the TV room and seems to have an idea.

HELEN EXITS.

LIGHTS FADE OFF

SCENE 4

THE 1975 – PLEASE BE NAKED BEGINS TO PLAY

LIGHTS FADE ON.

GRACE is in her room, getting ready for bed. She is in her own private room. She has a bed, a mirror and a few belongings from home, but it's hard to disguise the fact that it's a hospital room.

GRACE is putting away clothes and tidying up her room. She pulls out a hairbrush. For a while she stares at it. Then she throws it into the bin.

There is a knock at the door. Music stops playing. GRACE quickly pulls herself together and answers the door to see HELEN standing there.

HELEN: Grace! Let me in!

GRACE: Helen?

GRACE pulls the door open more so that she can let HELEN in.

HELEN: *(MUTTERING, TO HERSELF)* God, I hope no one saw me.

GRACE: What are you doing here?

HELEN: Give me a second… catch my breath.

GRACE: What's going on?

HELEN: Well, I've been thinking a lot about what you said today, in the TV room.

GRACE: Oh God, about the whole body shots and Dennis thing? Did I offend you?

HELEN: No, no, it wasn't that.

GRACE: All that stuff about the skin cancer? I was only joking, you know.

HELEN: No! No, it was nothing like that. You didn't offend me at all. Actually, sort of the opposite in a strange way.

GRACE: I don't understand.

HELEN: It was just everything you were saying about, you know, your party and missing out on all of these things that you should be looking forward to.

GRACE: Oh, God, please don't tell me that you feel sorry for me, because I will shove my bedpan so far up your arse.

HELEN: *(CHUCKLING)* No, no, I don't feel sorry for you. Actually, I wasn't even thinking about you.

GRACE: Charming.

HELEN: No, listen! You got me thinking about *me*.

GRACE: What?

HELEN: And then I was thinking about Rick. How we used to laugh and play and go dancing, back in the day. And I was thinking about Brett, and teaching him how to swim and ride a bike and giving him cuddles. I walked down the ward, past all of these people in the same situation, and just thought to myself, what are we doing? We're told we're sick, so we *act* sick? What about the days that we don't feel sick? What about the days that we can almost forget it's happening?

GRACE: That's called dementia, and that's another ward altogether.

HELEN: And then I was thinking about you.

GRACE: Me?

HELEN: Yes, you. You with your party and your Josh Green and that girl at school. Talking to you, you just don't care about all of… this. You won't let it stop you. You made me see that you're right.

GRACE: I am? About what?

HELEN: About living! You're so right, I can't believe that I couldn't see it before.

GRACE: Look, I'm glad you've had some kind of epiphany or whatever, Hel, but can't it wait until tomorrow? Oh I see… is this the new treatment? The stuff that made you a total bitch? Is it making you a bit loopy as well? Come on, Hel, let's get you back to bed, I'll ask the Doctor to get you a nice little brain scan…

HELEN: For Heaven's sake, girl, let me talk!

GRACE: Okay, okay, jeez.

HELEN: Finally. Now, get dressed.

GRACE: You what?

HELEN: Where's the outfit that you were going to wear to that party?

GRACE: Helen, what's going on?

HELEN: I want you to put on your party outfit. Get yourself all ready. I'm going to go and do the same. Then meet me in the TV room in ten minutes. Keep your head down, we don't want to draw any attention. Oh, and for once in your life, Grace, just shut up and do as you're told.

Completely taken aback, GRACE begins to do what HELEN says. HELEN leaves, a gleeful, mischievous look on her face.

SCENE 5

HELEN stands in the TV room, wearing a Santa hat and waiting for GRACE proudly. She has transformed the TV room into a Christmas party, with things that she has managed to find in the hospital - Throws, decorations, food, drink. There are little Christmas lights flashing different colours on the coffee table in the middle of the room. The TV is playing music from a channel called 'Christmas Hits of the 80s!'

GRACE enters. She is wearing a sparkly, very revealing outfit with a pair of antlers on her head.

GRACE: What the...

HELEN: Oh my goodness. Grace...

GRACE: What's all this?

HELEN: *(gesturing to GRACE's outfit)* What's all *this*?

GRACE: What? It's my party outfit. I'm a reindeer.

HELEN: And you look lovely, pet, but it's hardly low profile, is it?

GRACE: Oh well, we can cover for ourselves.

HELEN: Yes, well, at least something will be covering ourselves.

GRACE: Never mind that, what's going on? What *is* all this?

HELEN: Well, you didn't get to go to your party, did you? So here it is - the party has come to you!

GRACE: You did all this?

HELEN: Yup! I had these in my room, and then I managed to borrow some of the other things. We need to make sure we don't make too much of a mess, and be extra careful with everything of course, especially with Barry's lights, but...

She notices that GRACE is staring at her.

HELEN: Oh no. You hate it, don't you? Of course you do. I don't know what I was thinking. I know it's not exactly the fun night you wanted, and I'm not exactly Jess, but I thought that maybe it...

GRACE grabs HELEN and pulls her into an unexpected hug.

GRACE: It's... thank you.

HELEN: You're welcome.

They look at each other for a moment, emotional. GRACE pulls herself out of it first.

GRACE: I can't believe I have a private party just for me! This is gonna be wild!

HELEN: Well, we can't be too loud, and I wasn't exactly...

GRACE: *(INTERUPTING)* Alright, so we need a theme for this awesome party!

HELEN: Oh yes?

GRACE: I'm thinking maybe Christmas Divas? I'll be Mariah of course.

HELEN:	Don't worry, it's already taken care of!
GRACE:	It is? What's the theme?
HELEN:	This is… drum roll if you will, Grace.

GRACE does.

> Grace, welcome to your party… an 80s Christmas!

GRACE stops drumming abruptly.

GRACE:	I beg your pardon.
HELEN:	What?!
GRACE:	I'm sorry, I must have misheard you, I thought that you just said the 80s.
HELEN:	Yes, I did!
GRACE:	The 80's.
HELEN:	Yes!
GRACE:	As in… as in the *1*980's.
HELEN:	*(SIGHING)* Yes, Grace.
GRACE:	But… but the 80's were like… a gazillion years ago. This is like some kind of old peoples' event!
HELEN:	I'll have you know that the 80's were the best era ever. The music, the clothes, the hair, the John Hughes films, trousers so tight that you could barely breathe… it was all so brilliant.
GRACE:	Yeah, well, there's a reason that all of that stuff died out by the 90s.

HELEN: Come on, give it a go. If you're really not enjoying yourself within an hour, we can play your music and games.

GRACE: Brilliant, I have so much to introduce you to, Hel. Be prepared for Beer Pong and Olivia Rodrigo.

HELEN: Hmm, we'll see.

GRACE: Well, what are you waiting for, Hel? Turn it up, let's see what we're working with.

HELEN: Alright then.

HELEN turns up the music on the TV.

THE MUSIC GETS LOUDER. IT IS A COMPILATION OF 80s ICONS AND ICONIC CHRISTMAS SONGS, INCLUDING BAND AID, WHAM!, THE POGUES ETC.

In a sequence underlined by various 80s hits, we see GRACE and HELEN dancing, singing along, partying and playing. They dress up in various things that HELEN has managed to source such as fluorescent beads and both play party games. They are having the time of their lives, both introducing each other to new things.

Eventually, they collapse in their chairs, out of breath and laughing.

BAND AID 'DO THEY KNOW IT'S CHRISTMAS' PLAYS as they sit down. It continues to play in the background of the scene.

GRACE: Ah, tune! Dance with me, Hel!

HELEN: Give me a minute, love, I'm knackered.

They both sit for a moment, catching their breath. They catch eyes and burst out laughing again at the sight of one another. HELEN wipes tears of laughter from her face.

HELEN: Oh dear!

GRACE: WHAT a night!

HELEN: I know!

GRACE: I'm actually sweating.

HELEN: Me too, I don't think I've danced like that in years!

GRACE: I can't believe how amazing this music is! I'm gonna watch this channel more. That George Michael guy was well fit as well, I would have deffo fancied him back in the day.

HELEN: Yeah, about him…

GRACE: Oh you were so right, Hel! I can't believe how cool this is!

HELEN: I'm glad you're having fun.

GRACE: Aren't you?

HELEN: I am. I really, honestly am.

GRACE: You suck at beer pong, though.

HELEN: I know! I'm just grateful that it wasn't really beer.

GRACE: Yeah, that's the only thing you missed out on, Hel. The alcohol.

HELEN: Who needs it?

GRACE: I guess. Still, next time I'm gonna get you so wasted.

HELEN: Next time?

GRACE: Yeah! When we're both out of here. We'll go to a real 80s tribute night at one of those crummy community centres filled with oldies trying to recapture their youth.

HELEN: Grace.

GRACE: Sorry! I don't mean you, obviously.

HELEN: How reassuring.

GRACE: But we will, won't we, Hel? We'll go and we'll dance and we'll sing and we'll dress up. Can we, please?

HELEN: I'd love that.

GRACE: Amazing. We'll plan it, the second we're out.

HELEN: It's a deal.

GRACE: Thank you so much, Helen.

HELEN: That's alright, love.

GRACE: No, I mean it. Thank you. For everything. This might be the best night of my whole life.

HELEN: Me too, actually.

GRACE: What? You can't say that! What about your wedding night? Or the night that Brett was born?!

HELEN: Brett didn't come out with a mullet singing Duran Duran!

THEY LAUGH.

You know, we should probably go back.

GRACE: Back?

HELEN: To bed. We can't hide in here for too long, people will be coming round soon.

GRACE: Ugh, I know. It's just not fair.

HELEN: I know.

GRACE: I just wish it could be like this all the time.

HELEN: I know, I know. But it will be like this for you all the time, soon.

GRACE: Do you think?

HELEN: Definitely. Trust me, Grace, if there's anyone out there who could come out of all of this fighting, it's you.

GRACE: *(VISIBLY TOUCHED)* You know that you're coming with me.

HELEN: Why of course, we have that double act to be getting on with, don't we?

GRACE: Oh yes, Philip and Holly part 2.

HELEN: Only if I get Phil!

GRACE: *(LAUGHING)* Deal. Right then. I suppose we need to go.

HELEN: Yes, I guess you're right.

GRACE: We need to tidy up all this stuff.

HELEN: I'll do it. Where's the remote?

HELEN goes to turn off the television.

THE SOUND OF CYNDI LAUPER'S 'GIRLS JUST WANNA HAVE FUN' starts to play.

GRACE and HELEN look at each other.

HELEN: It couldn't hurt to stay for just *one* more song.

GRACE: Yay!

GRACE leaps up on the chair and begins to act out the song, making HELEN laugh. HELEN plays along.

GRACE: *(SINGING)* Girls, just wanna be stage one. Girls, just wanna be stage one!

HELEN: *(her laughing coming to a hesitant stop)* What?

GRACE: I'm just playing, Hel, come on, next verse!

GRACE jumps up and carries on singing. HELEN turns down the music.

GRACE: Hey! I'm not done!

HELEN: What do you mean, stage one? Aren't you stage one?

GRACE: Just leave it, Hel, I was only messing around.

HELEN: Grace.

GRACE: Oh, for God's sake, Hel, don't ruin the party.

HELEN: Grace, this is serious. Talk to me!

GRACE: About what?!

HELEN: Are you stage one?

GRACE: What does it matter? It doesn't change anything.

HELEN: You know that it does! Now stop acting like a child and talk to me!

GRACE: A child? Are you for real right now?

HELEN: You're acting like one!

GRACE: Woah, hang on just a minute! Sorry, are you suddenly my Mother or my Doctor now? Because the last time that I checked, I thought that you were supposed to be my friend.

HELEN: I *am* your friend, Grace, but...

GRACE: But nothing, Hel. You're acting like a right old bore and I don't need it. I get enough lecturing from my parents and from the hospital and I don't need it from you!

HELEN: Just tell me, what stage are you?

GRACE: I don't see how that's important.

HELEN: Just tell me, Grace!

GRACE: Three!!

There is a shocked silence and stillness.

GRACE: Three. I'm stage three.

HELEN: Three. But... But you didn't say. I thought you were stage one?

GRACE: I was. A while ago.

HELEN: I can't believe you didn't tell me.

GRACE: I told you enough.

HELEN: You told me that your treatment hadn't worked the way that the Doctors had wanted, but you didn't tell me what that actually meant. You're susceptible to infection at the moment, Grace. Really susceptible. One little cold could really screw up your immune system and trigger something. And you let me do all of this in here! It's filled with germs and it's all dirty and sticky and... and...

GRACE: And brilliant! And beautiful and colourful and fucking *alive!* Don't you get it, Hel? Everyone is always trying to wrap me up in cotton wool.

HELEN: We're all trying to protect you...

GRACE: What do you know about protecting me? You don't know anything about me!

HELEN: I know a great deal more than you think, young lady, I'm...

GRACE: *Young lady?!* Could you sound any more patronising if you tried? Who do you think you are, trying to tell me what to do?

HELEN: I'm a 65 year old woman. I've lived a whole life and I've learnt a lot along the way, and I'm sorry to say that means that I know a lot more than you. And yes. Yes. I have cancer. It wasn't part of the plan and I don't know what it means, but I know that I'm bloody petrified. As mundane, and insignificant and *ordinary* as my little life is, it's mine, and I love it. I love my boy and I love meeting up with old friends for a cup of tea and a slice of cake whilst moaning that I'm not getting any thinner and I love sitting with a bottle of wine and watching my programmes at the weekend. I'm not ready to let it all go, not yet, and I'm terrified of losing everything. For a while, I couldn't face up to it. I didn't want to even think about it. But being with you, watching you pretend that you're fine, whilst knowing that one cold could kill you… it's made me see that we can't keep burying our head in the sand. We need to face up to it. We need to accept that we're ill and we need to hope to God that we get better.

GRACE: You're so clueless.

HELEN: I beg your pardon?!

GRACE: You don't get it! You don't get any of it, do you? I'm not ignoring my illness, Helen. I can never forget that I'm the leukaemia girl. It's like I have it strapped to my head in massive fucking flashing letters.

HELEN: Then how can you be so reckless?

GRACE: Because it's suffocating me! This, all of this! It's too much! This is why I didn't tell you. You're treating me differently already now that you know.

HELEN: Of course I'm treating you differently! I'm trying to protect you! Stage I, it's low risk, the survival rates, they're... but, Grace, Stage III...

GRACE: This is what I'm saying! I don't want this! I don't want to talk about it anymore.

HELEN: Oh what, so you're just going to ignore it? You're just going to do what you always do, make a funny joke, make an inappropriate comment and hope nobody knows the truth?

GRACE: I'm dying!

HELEN stares at her, shocked into silence.

GRACE: Is that what you want to hear, Helen? That I'm dying? Do you think I don't know? Do you think I don't hear what all of the Doctors say? Do you think I don't know that people whisper behind my back, feeling sorry for me? Do you think I haven't googled every single fucking thing about my condition? Of course I have. Of course I know what's going to happen. When I had it before, when I was little it was different. I knew I'd get better, everyone said I would get better and I did. But then it came back. And this time, I know it's not going away. I'm going to die. It's as simple as that. We can keep pretending, keep pretending that the treatments will work, that putting me here, in the private section of the Marsen will help, that this time, *this time*, this round of chemo and radio will miraculously work and I'll be better, because oh I'm so young, and oh, isn't it so unfair? But why should I keep getting my hopes up? I've accepted it. Why can't everybody else?

HELEN: Grace...

GRACE: Thinking about it. Talking about it. Dwelling on it... It's like somebody squeezing on my skull, their fingers digging in until my brain explodes. I can't stand it. I don't want to think about it. I know how I feel inside and I know that, right now, I'm still here. I'm here and I'm talking, and eating, and walking and breathing - but I'm not *feeling*. For the last few years, I've missed out on everything, Helen. When a new film comes out in the cinema and I think to myself, I'd love to go and see that, I fucking can't. I can't just go Christmas shopping or go for drinks or even get on a fucking bus or pet a dog in the street or run out to the shop because I'm hungry and I fancy biscuits. Everyone's been so focussed on making sure that I don't die that they've forgotten to let me *live*.

HELEN: I'm sorry, Grace. I can't watch you do this.

GRACE: Helen.

HELEN: I'm sorry.

HELEN walks off. GRACE stands on the stage alone, watching her go.

GRACE: Well, fuck you then!

GRACE sits down on her usual chair, deflated.

(WHISPERS) Fuck you.

GRACE puts her head into her hands and starts to cry.

SCENE 6

BLUE BY FIRST AID KIT PLAYS.

LIGHTS FADE UP.

HELEN walks onto the stage. Time has gone by since her argument with GRACE. She looks unhappy and lost.

She sits in the TV room. She looks up at the door a few times, as though waiting for somebody to walk through it - but nobody does.

She gets up and takes in the TV room, half-heartedly trying to start a variety of activities, such as watch TV, do a crossword or make a cup of tea, but remains too distracted.

HELEN EXITS.

GRACE ENTERS.

GRACE walks in, as though expecting to see HELEN and like she has something important to say. When she realises that she's not there, she hesitates, before decided to leave.

GRACE EXITS.

HELEN ENTERS.

HELEN enters, holding a piece of paper, reading it anxiously over and over. She is clearly trying to come to terms with something. She pulls out her phone multiple times, as though to make a call, but doesn't quite manage it. We watch her have an internal battle with herself. She finally plucks up the courage to make the call and leaves.

HELEN EXITS.

GRACE ENTERS.

GRACE comes in, this time to fill up a hot water bottle. She could have done this with the kettle in her room, but has decided to come in here with the hope of seeing HELEN. GRACE looks more unwell that she has done previously. She is getting slightly greyer, slower and more downbeat – although we don't know how much of this is her illness and how much is the argument with HELEN. We see GRACE wearily resting in the room, drinking water and taking deep breaths, as though she feels sick. When the kettle boils, GRACE fills up the hot water bottle, then leaves to go back to bed.

GRACE EXITS.

BLUE BY FIRST AID KIT STOPS PLAYING

HELEN ENTERS.

HELEN is finishing up her phone call.

HELEN: *(on the phone)* Of course, love, of course. No, Brett, honestly, please don't come. I just wanted to tell you… Okay. Listen. You know that they needed to do those tests? Yes, they're about to come back. Tomorrow. I just wanted to tell you, you know… just in case… no, I can't… no. Yes, I'll give you a ring straight away. Okay, okay. Of course we will, love… yes, yes. I love you too, Brett. So much. Bye. Bye.

HELEN hangs up. She looks tearful. She takes a moment to compose herself before leaving.

LIGHTS OFF.

SCENE 7

LIGHTS UP.

SOUNDS OF A TV PROGRAMME PLAY IN THE BACKGROUND.

GRACE is sitting in the TV room in her usual chair. She has her legs up and is holding a cup of tea. She is watching a TV Programme. She is dressed in comfortable clothes and hugging the hot water bottle. She looks and feels a bit better than in the previous scene, but is still unwell.

HELEN walks in, hesitating when she spots GRACE sitting there.

GRACE glances up and sees HELEN. The pair exchange an awkward glance. It is reminiscent of their first encounter.

HELEN starts to make a cup of tea, stealing glances at GRACE every so often. GRACE keeps her eyes on the floor, on the TV – anywhere but on HELEN.

HELEN tentatively walks over and sits next to GRACE. She brings with her a cup of tea and a plate of biscuits, which she puts down between them. GRACE gives both the biscuits and HELEN a sideward glance, but does not say anything. HELEN begins to watch TV with her. They don't look at or speak to one another.

THERE IS THE SFX OF A PRESENTER ON THE TV ANNOUNCING:

'And next we move onto today's documentary, Britain's top 100 dogs.'

GRACE and HELEN react to this. They shift awkwardly in their chairs.

As the documentary progresses, they become more restless, stealing glances at one another and suppressing girlish giggles

THERE IS THE SFX OF THE PRESENTER ON THE TV ANNOUNCING:

'We think we know our dogs – but how can we know exactly what they're thinking?'

GRACE and HELEN both look at each other and break out into laughter.

HELEN: Grace...

GRACE: *(THROWING HER ARMS AROUND HELEN)* I'm sorry, Hel / I'm so, so sorry!

HELEN: / I'm sorry too!

GRACE: I shouldn't have shouted at you like that.

HELEN: No, no, it was my fault. I had no right to get involved in your business like that.

GRACE: No, it's okay, honestly, I know that you were just looking out for me.

HELEN smiles at her, gratefully.

GRACE: Helen. I'm sorry that I didn't tell you.

HELEN: *(GENTLY)* You don't have anything to be sorry for.

GRACE: Well, I am.

There is a brief, awkward PAUSE.

HELEN: Are you, you know. Okay?

GRACE: Yeah, yeah, good, thanks. You?

HELEN: Yeah, yeah, good, thanks.

They smile at one another, somewhat shyly.

GRACE: So what have I missed?

HELEN: *(FLUSTERED)* What? Oh, um, not a lot… you know… nothing exciting… why do you ask?

GRACE: It just feels like forever since our night! I have *loads* to fill you in on. Do you really not have any goss?

HELEN: No… no. Nothing. Nothing.

GRACE: Poor you.

HELEN: So, tell me all of your news then.

GRACE: Where to start?! Okay, so, Jess called me after that night we had, 'cos you know, she went to that party that I wanted to go to? So yeah, I told her all about our night and she said that our night sounded *way* more fun than the party, so she was totally jel of that. Imagine, getting jealous of a night that I had in here! Anyway, she said that she had some proper juicy goss for me, right? So I was like, Oh God, what did you do now, because you know what Jess is like… well actually, you don't know, but anyway, she said that it wasn't her at all, but you know Luce? The girl who was hosting the party, the model wannabe? Well apparently she got off with Jason!

GRACE PAUSES DRAMATICALLY. She looks at HELEN for a reaction, who stares back at her, blankly.

GRACE: Right, well, obviously you don't know Jason, but he was like, this proper, like, *lad* lad from school if you know what I mean who got with literally everyone - but anyway - so he was making out with Luce but *then* her *boyfriend*, Joel shows up, and apparently it all just went totally mad. There was this huge fight, right, so the police get called out and THEN while all of that was going on, a girl called Vicky, you don't know her either, she's cool, but she was on the trampoline while it was all kicking off and she was totally wasted and she fell off and broke her arm, so the ambulance came out as well. Jess said that everyone had to go down to the local park and freeze their arse's off just waiting to sober up before they went home so the police didn't see them. It sounds like it was a proper mess. I'm actually so glad I didn't go. I wasn't meant to talk about it though, because of the police and that, so don't say anything, okay?

HELEN: …I couldn't even if I wanted to, love.

GRACE: So yeah, that's pretty much it.

HELEN: That's all your news? Nothing else?

GRACE: Yeah pretty much. I'm just so excited. It's nearly Christmas, Hel! I can't wait! Mum, Dad and Jess are coming over in the morning, and I think a load of my other friends and family want to stop by at some point. But Dr Cook is being a right bitch and she said that only three people can come because of infections and shit.

HELEN: Well… maybe she's right.

GRACE glares at her. HELEN backtracks quickly.

HELEN: But then again, maybe she's not.

GRACE: Damn right she's not. She's not ruining Christmas no fucking way. It's Jesus' birthday after all and I'm gonna have the party he deserves. I'm having the full works: tons of presents, snuck-in booze, cake, the lot.

HELEN: What was that second one?

GRACE: Cake?

HELEN: Sure. *(laughing)* Sounds like it will be brilliant, love.

GRACE: It really will be. I just can't wait! You're going to come by and meet everyone, right?

HELEN: *(VISIBLY UNCOMFORTABLE)* Oh, I wouldn't want to intrude on your day with your family and Jess, love. But I'll pop by at some point.

GRACE: Of course you wouldn't be intruding, *you're* family! You gotta spend time with family at Christmas.

HELEN is taken aback and touched by that.

GRACE: What's the best present you've ever gotten?

HELEN: Goodness, I'm not sure! I can't really remember the best. I've had a lot of lovely gifts.

GRACE: Go on then, what's the worst? Brett must have got you something shit when he was little, right?

HELEN: No! Every gift is special, because it was from him.

GRACE: Ugh, bore. What about Rick?

HELEN: Oh well, now that's a different story.

GRACE: Knew it! Go on, what did he get?

HELEN: Well... there was one year... and he meant well I guess but... he just doesn't listen, I'd told him I wanted this new watch, but he just... ugh...

GRACE: Yeah, yeah, go on, what was it?

HELEN: Well... he got me an oven glove.

GRACE opens her mouth in shock before doubling over, laughing.

GRACE: Oh my God! I bet you were fuming! No wonder you divorced him!

GRACE howls with laughter. HELEN allows herself a giggle

HELEN: I wasn't happy, that's for sure.

GRACE: I promise to get you something better, Hel, when I'm finally out of here, I'll go shopping especially.

There is a pause as they both reflect on that statement and the reality that GRACE probably will never get to do that. GRACE looks pained, and HELEN decides to play along.

HELEN: Of course you will.

GRACE smiles gratefully.

GRACE: So do you still use it?

HELEN: Use what?

GRACE: Your special oven glove?

HELEN: Oh no, it fell apart years ago.

GRACE: Oh well, nothing lasts forever. Anyway, I'm gonna go. I need to go beg bitchface to let more people come visit for my Christmas do.

HELEN: Grace...

GRACE: Sorry. Doctor Cook.

HELEN: Alright then, love.

GRACE stands up to leave. She stops and looks at HELEN.

GRACE: Helen?

HELEN: Hmmm?

GRACE: I'm really glad we're friends again.

HELEN: Me too, love.

They smile at one another.

GRACE EXITS.

HELEN watches after GRACE, thoughtfully.

HELEN pulls out her phone. She looks as though she has a million thoughts racing through her head.

HELEN: Brett? I got the results.

BLACKOUT.

SCENE 8

LIGHTS FADE ON

GRACE wakes up in her room. It is finally Christmas day. She sits up on the bed, excitedly, and grabs a pile of cards and presents. She rips into them.

GRACE'S PHONE RINGS.

GRACE answers the phone.

GRACE: HELLO? JESSY!

SHE LAUGHS

GRACE: Merry Christmas right back at you! You what? Yeah, deffo! You'd better bring some later! What time do you think you'll get here? *(Listening)* What… sorry what about Tommy and Beth? Oh… I don't know, I didn't hear… they did? When? Oh… okay right… of course… well maybe just Beth could… did he? Oh that's great… yeah, I'm happy for you! Well he can come by later as well if he wants… oh yeah, no… it's okay, I get it… of course you do…

GRACE begins to tear up. She tries to interject into the conversation every now and again, but it is obvious she is not listening to what JESS is saying.

GRACE: Uh-huh… what? Yeah, course. Yeah, alright, yeah sure, see you then. Yeah, they'll be here any minute, so… alright… okay… yeah thanks anyway. Yeah, you too. Bye.

GRACE hangs up the phone. She sits silently.

GRACE'S PHONE BEGINS TO RING AGAIN.

GRACE composes herself, plastering a smile onto her face as she answers the phone.

GRACE: Hello? Hey, Mum. Merry Christmas! I know! Yeah, I'll be ready in five, are you nearly here? Okay, I'll see you in a sec! Okay, bye!

GRACE puts the phone down and wipes her eyes. She picks up a Christmas jumper and holds it against her. She looks into the mirror and forces a smile onto her face.

LIGHTS FADE OUT.

SCENE 9

THE LIGHTS FADE UP.

It is the afternoon of Christmas day. GRACE and HELEN are sitting in their usual chairs in the TV room. They are both wearing Christmas jumpers. GRACE is wearing her antlers and HELEN is wearing her Santa hat. They are eating Christmas cakes.

GRACE: *(THROUGH A MOUTHFUL OF CAKE)* Okay, wait, I've got a good one.

HELEN: Okay, I'm ready.

GRACE: Alright, where's the wildest place that you've ever done 'it'?

HELEN: *(LAUGHING)* Grace!

GRACE: What? I have to live vicariously. Let me tell you all of this puking and swelling isn't exactly a major turn-on.

HELEN: Well now… I suppose… that depends on which one of you is doing the swelling…

GRACE: YES Helen! This is what I've been waiting for! I knew you were a saucy old minx after all!

HELEN: I can't believe I just said that! I think it's your bad influence!

GRACE: Well then, my work here is done. So go on then, your wildest place?

HELEN: Oh God, no, I can't.

GRACE: Pleeeeaaaaseee, it's Christmas!

HELEN: Alright, alright! Pfft, wildest place? Okay, yes, I've got one.

GRACE: *(GIGGLING)* Yeah?

HELEN: *(ALSO GIGGLING)* Yeah.

GRACE: Okay, so go on then!

HELEN: Okay... so... ah, I cannot BELEVE I am telling you this... but once... my ex-husband and I... well, you know... back in the day... we could be a bit... you know... so this one time, we came home, and we had been drinking you know?

GRACE: Yeah...

HELEN: And we were already a bit, you know, excited like...

GRACE: Uh-huh...

HELEN: And so we got in and we couldn't wait... it was like a film or something... and we ended up doing it... on the sofa... downstairs!

HELEN laughs, thrilled with this reveal. GRACE stares at her.

There is a PAUSE.

GRACE: The sofa?

HELEN: Yes!

GRACE: Downstairs? In your house?

HELEN: Yes!

GRACE: ...Wow. Saucy.

HELEN: I'll have you know that Brett could have walked in and caught us at any moment! It was all rather exciting actually.

GRACE: *(tucking back into her cake)* Tell you what, Hel, once you get out of here I'm gonna help you to get some proper juicy stories. God knows, you need it.

HELEN is silent for a moment. She looks awkward, like she has something that she needs to say, but does not. Instead, she asks a different question.

HELEN: So, did you have a good morning with your parents?

GRACE: Oh Hel, it was so nice, they came and they had a proper stocking and a bunch of decorations and stuff. They spoilt me too, tons of presents. You should have come and said hi.

HELEN: Oh, I didn't want to interfere.

GRACE: Course you wouldn't have, silly. You can see them later anyway, they're coming back this evening.

HELEN: Well, we'll see. Have you had any other presents?

GRACE: Yeah, the nurses on the ward gave me a gorgeous jumper from New Look and Jess is gonna bring me her present next week.

HELEN: Next week? She isn't coming over today?

GRACE: No. New boyfriend, surprised her dressed as a Sexy Santa apparently. I don't know him.

HELEN: Couldn't he come to visit too?

GRACE: Yes. You'd think so.

There is a bit of an awkward PAUSE.

GRACE: So, are you going to come?

HELEN: Hmm?

GRACE: Hello? To my room later, to meet Mum and Dad?

HELEN: Oh, right.

GRACE: Bloody hell, you really are on another planet today. I bet it's from that crappy Christmas dinner they served us, I told you that turkey smelt funny.

HELEN: Sorry... well no, I can't come over, love. You see... the thing is... well Brett's coming.

GRACE: Well that's okay, he can come and say hi too. I can't wait to meet him.

HELEN: That's very kind, love, but Brett and I are actually going to be really busy... you see the thing is... he's sort of helping me to pack up all of my things.

GRACE: Pack up? Why, where are yo-... (*she trails of as realisation hits her.*) Oh my God... no way... it hasn't... has it...

HELEN: (*Nodding*) For now.

GRACE: When? What? How?

HELEN: A few weeks ago, after our night, a specialist came in and ran some tests. I didn't think much of it until they called me in for a meeting a few days ago. I thought they were going to say... well, it doesn't matter what I thought. I'm carrying on with the treatment and I'll obviously be doing regularly check-ups and there's no certainty for the future of course, but for now... I'm all clear.

SILENCE

Are you okay? I'm sorry, I hope you're not upset, I wanted to tell you, but it's Christmas and I didn't want...

GRACE drops her plate of cake, letting it fall to the floor. She leaps out of her chair and throws her arms around HELEN.

GRACE: Don't be silly! This is amazing! I'm so, so happy!

The pair hug for a while, holding each other tightly. When they break away, they are both teary-eyed. HELEN gets out a tissue and passes it to GRACE.

HELEN: Goodness, just look at us.

GRACE: How long are you staying for?

HELEN: Until tomorrow. I'm sorry to tell you today.

GRACE: No, it's honestly so brilliant! It's the best present I could have hoped for!

There is a PAUSE.

You got me a real present as well though, right?!

HELEN: *(LAUGHING)* Brett's bringing it with him later. I'll give it to you tomorrow, before I leave.

GRACE: Okay, cool. Shall we meet in here?

HELEN: Here sounds perfect.

GRACE: Great.

There is a brief silence as the pair reflect.

HELEN: Do you remember the first thing you said to me?

GRACE: Something rude probably, my Mum's always saying that I have no filter.

HELEN: No, you asked me if dogs thought in barks.

GRACE: Oh yeah! We were in these chairs, watching that documentary.

HELEN: I thought you were completely mad.

GRACE: I thought you were a stuck up old cow.

LAUGHTER THEN SILENCE.

GRACE: What am I going to do without you?

HELEN: Hey now, what's all that about? You'll be great!

GRACE: But we've had so much fun together. Truth be told, Hel, things were pretty shit until I met you. You kind of my saved my arse there. I might have died of boredom before the leukaemia got me.

HELEN: *(CHOKING UP)* I know, love. God, I know. But it was the other way around, Grace. You saved me. You showed me how to live again. I can't remember the last time I had real, honest-to-God, childish fun before I met you.

GRACE: I am pretty fun.

HELEN: That you are, love.

GRACE: It's gonna suck without you here.

HELEN: But I'll be here all the time. I have to come in for check-ups and I was thinking that we could pick a day every week to have as our TV day and I'll come and visit you. I can come in and we can just watch TV and eat cake and…

GRACE: Talk about your wild times on a sofa?

HELEN: And talk about anything other than that!

They laugh. There is a brief PAUSE.

GRACE: Helen?

HELEN: Hmmm?

GRACE: I'm so happy for you.

HELEN: I know, love.

ANOTHER PAUSE.

GRACE: Hey, Hel?

HELEN: Yes, Grace?

GRACE: How do you reckon a dog would think, 'I love you?'

HELEN: Ooh, well, I suppose he'd think, 'Bark bark bark.'

GRACE: Oh right yeah. In that case, Bark bark bark, Helen.

HELEN: Bark bark bark, Grace.

PAUSE.

GRACE: So, do you have to go right away, or do you have some time?

HELEN: I've got some time, Brett won't be here for a while.

GRACE: Great… well… do you wanna watch some TV?

HELEN: Sounds perfect.

GRACE reaches for the remote and switches on the TV.

GRACE: Merry Christmas, Hel.

HELEN: Merry Christmas, Grace.

We hear the sound of the TV switching on and the pair settling down to watch it. The sounds of a nature documentary are heard.

HELEN and GRACE glance up at each-other and smile.
BLACKOUT. **END**